EVERYDAY STEM

HOW SELF-DRIVING
CARS WORK

IAN CHOW-MILLER

Cavendish
Square

MATTESON AREA PUBLIC LIBRARY
DISTRICT

New York

Published in 2019 by Cavendish Square Publishing, LLC
243 5th Avenue, Suite 136, New York, NY 10016

Copyright © 2019 by Cavendish Square Publishing, LLC

First Edition

No part of this publication may be reproduced, stored in a retrieval system, or transmitted in any form or by any means—electronic, mechanical, photocopying, recording, or otherwise—without the prior permission of the copyright owner. Request for permission should be addressed to Permissions, Cavendish Square Publishing, 243 5th Avenue, Suite 136, New York, NY 10016. Tel (877) 980-4450; fax (877) 980-4454.

Website: cavendishsq.com

This publication represents the opinions and views of the author based on his or her personal experience, knowledge, and research. The information in this book serves as a general guide only. The author and publisher have used their best efforts in preparing this book and disclaim liability rising directly or indirectly from the use and application of this book.

All websites were available and accurate when this book was sent to press.

Library of Congress Cataloging-in-Publication Data

Names: Chow-Miller, Ian, author.
Title: How self-driving cars work / Ian Chow-Miller.
Description: First edition. | New York : Cavendish Square, 2019. | Series: Everyday STEM |
Includes index. | Audience: Grades 2-5. | Identifiers: LCCN 2017053340 (print) |
LCCN 2017056357 (ebook) | ISBN 9781502637512 (ebook) | ISBN 9781502637482 (library bound) |
ISBN 9781502637499 (pbk.) | ISBN 9781502637505 (6 pack)
Subjects: LCSH: Autonomous vehicles--Juvenile literature. |
Autonomous vehicles--Design and construction--Juvenile literature. |
Automobiles--Automatic control--Juvenile literature. | CYAC: Autonomous vehicles. | Automobiles.
Classification: LCC TL152.8 (ebook) | LCC TL152.8 .C46 2019 (print) | DDC 629.2--dc23
LC record available at https://lccn.loc.gov/2017053340

Editorial Director: David McNamara
Editor: Meghan Lamb
Copy Editor: Nathan Heidelberger
Associate Art Director: Amy Greenan
Designer: Christina Shults
Production Coordinator: Karol Szymczuk
Photo Research: J8 Media

The photographs in this book are used by permission and through the courtesy of:
Cover Brooks Kraft LLC/Corbis/Getty Images; p. 4 Matt Henry Gunther/The Image Bank/Getty Images; p. Chronicle/Alamy Stock Photo; p. 8 Innovatedcaptures/iStock/Thinkstock; p. 9 RobertCrum/iStock/Thinkstock; p. 10 Simon Dawson/Bloomberg/Getty Images; p. 12 Bloomberg/Getty Images; p. 14 Yaoinlove/Shutterstock. com; p. 17 Chombosan/iStock/Thinkstock; p. 18 Glenn Chapman/AFP/Getty Images; p. 21 David McNew/ Getty Images; p. 22 Victor Habbick Visions/Science Photo Library/Getty Images; p. 23 AFP/Getty Images; p. 24 Chombosan/Shutterstock.com;p. 26 DaCek/Shutterstock.com;p. 27 Jeffrey Blackler/Alamy Stock Photo.

Printed in the United States of America

CONTENTS

THE RECOMMENDED MINIMUM TIRE AIR
PRESSURE FOR THIS POWER VEHICLE IS:

030269

School buses are one of many driver-operated
vehicles you see on the road.

CHAPTER 1
WHAT IS A SELF-DRIVING CAR?

Imagine all the cars, trucks, and buses moving down a busy street. What do they all have in common? They all have a person driving in the front seat. They all have pedals to make them go. They all have brakes to make them stop. They all have steering wheels to make them turn left and right.

Very soon, this may change. Companies are making cars that drive themselves. These cars do not need a person to drive them. Many do not even need steering wheels!

DIFFERENT KINDS OF SELF-DRIVING CARS

Not all self-driving cars work all by themselves. Some need the driver to help control their movement. The amount of control a car has over its movement is

General Motors was one of the first companies to design self-driving cars.

HOW SELF-DRIVING CARS WORK

WHO FIRST IMAGINED SELF-DRIVING CARS?

The first person to imagine a city with driverless cars was Norman Bel Geddes. Geddes showed his idea at the World's Fair in 1939. The car company General Motors liked Geddes's idea. In 1958, General Motors made a 400-foot (122-meter) section of highway with electrical wires built into the road. A car with a special machine that could detect the electricity in these wires was able to drive down the road with the driver keeping his hands off the steering wheel. The car was even able to follow a turn in the road, without any human steering!

Google designed the front of its self-driving car to look like a smiling face. They wanted people to feel relaxed when they saw a car without a driver.

called **autonomy**. Some self-driving cars have a lot of autonomy. Some have only a little.

A car with full autonomy drives itself without any

Humans often make mistakes that lead to car accidents.

Thousands of car accidents happen every day. Some can be minor. Others can be quite bad.

help. The passenger can take his or her hands off the steering wheel. He or she doesn't have to watch the road.

In cars with full autonomy, there is no driver. There is no steering wheel. There are no pedals or brakes. The self-driving car does not need them. The car can start, stop, speed up, slow down, turn, and park on its own.

Some self-driving cars do not have full autonomy. These cars use **assistive** devices. This means the car assists (or helps) the driver. It does this by warning the driver when there might be an accident. If another car gets too close, the

There will be no need for steering wheels in self-driving cars.

assistive device will beep. The loud noise warns the driver. The driver needs to slow down the car or steer away from danger.

WHY THERE ARE DIFFERENT KINDS OF SELF-DRIVING CARS

People have been driving cars for more than one hundred years. For all that time, drivers have

While there may not be many self-driving cars on the road yet, there are more and more each year. Some scientists predict that the majority of cars on the road will be self-driving by 2030.

Some self-driving cars can show you maps of the road ahead.

been in control. Being in control gives people a feeling of safety. When people are not in control, they might feel helpless or nervous. It may take people a long time to get used to cars that control themselves. It may take a long time for people to feel safe in self-driving cars.

That is why companies make cars with different levels of control. They want to help people get used to cars that do work people have always done themselves. They want to help people feel comfortable in cars with more autonomy.

Like cell phones, self-driving cars use GPS, which stands for "Global Positioning System."

CHAPTER 2
HOW DO SELF-DRIVING CARS WORK?

Have you ever heard a cell phone telling a driver where to go? A computer program inside the phone lets it do this. This program works using **GPS**, which stands for "Global Positioning System."

The GPS in a cell phone works by receiving signals sent from satellites in space. Satellites are manmade objects that **orbit** Earth. This means they float around Earth all the time, moving at a steady speed. The phone compares the signals from three different satellites. This lets it locate itself (and the car) on a map. The phone uses GPS to track the car on the map as it moves. It gives directions to help the driver get around.

FAST FACT

At first, traffic might get worse when we have a lot of self-driving cars on the road. These cars will be slow at traffic lights because they want to be safe. However, self-driving cars are able to learn over time and make better decisions.

In a self-driving car, there is no need to use your phone. A computer with a GPS program is built into the car. The computer controls the GPS. Computers coordinate all the systems that help drive driverless cars. "Coordinate" means "work together."

A self-driving car uses many different sensors to detect its surroundings.

SENSING THE ENVIRONMENT

To drive safely, the self-driving car must avoid dangers that come into its path. Dangers include other cars, animals, or human beings.

Self-driving cars use all of their sensors to generate accurate pictures of their surroundings.

A self-driving car needs to know the difference between a bicycle and a motorcycle. It needs to know when it is driving up to a stoplight or a stop sign. When a self-driving car pulls into a parking space, it needs to know no one is standing in the space. How does the driverless car know all of these things? It uses information from sensors.

Sensors are objects that "sense" information about the environment and send that information to a computer. Sensors are similar to the parts on your body that sense: your ears hear sounds, and your eyes see images. There are sensors on self-driving cars that use sounds and images as well. One type of sensor that a self-driving car uses is called **lidar**. "Lidar" stands for "Light Detection and Ranging."

Lidar shoots out a laser in thousands of quick bursts, or pulses, every few seconds. These laser

PROS AND CONS

In 2014, there were approximately thirty-two thousand deaths from car crashes. Ninety-four percent of those deaths were due to mistakes or bad choices people made while driving. Self-driving cars are safer because they don't make bad choices or mistakes. Even so, there are still some concerns about self-driving cars.

One argument is that these cars will take away jobs. For example, if we had self-driving trucks and buses, they would put all the bus drivers and truck drivers out of business. Another problem is figuring out who is at fault if there is an accident. There is no driver to blame. Should you blame the car's owner, the passenger, or the company that made the car? These questions must be answered before self-driving cars become common.

pulses are invisible
and can't hurt people.
They are different
from laser guns you
may have seen on TV.
These invisible pulses
hit objects all around
the car, including

A lidar sensor system is mounted on the top of this car.

trees, buildings, and people. Then, the sensor waits for those pulses to bounce back to the car. The computer times how long it takes these pulses to return to the car. The faster the signals come back, the closer an object is.

Sonar (Sound Navigation and Ranging) is another type of sensor. Sonar is similar to the **echolocation** used by animals like bats and

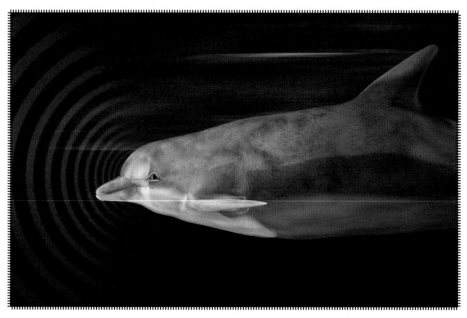
Dolphins use echolocation just like self-driving cars use sonar.

dolphins to find their way. Sonar technology is also similar to lidar. Instead of using laser pulses like lidar, however, sonar uses sound waves to locate objects. These sound waves are too high for humans to hear—but the sonar can detect them.

Coordinating Sensors

Self-driving cars need to be safe. They need to use many different types of sensors. Sonar, lidar, and GPS coordinate to tell the self-driving car where it is and what is around it.

This coordination is important because each sensor has a different job it is really good at.

Cameras and other sensors can also be mounted to the top of a car.

Sonar works well at close ranges. It can help cars pull into a parking spot without hitting anything. Lidar is really good at generating 360-degree maps of the area around the car. These maps tell the car what is on the road ahead of you, behind you, and to your sides for as far as

Cameras are used to help tell the difference between trucks, cars, and other vehicles.

650 feet (200 meters) in all directions. And while lidar can detect signs and traffic lights, self-driving cars use cameras to tell what color the traffic light is or what type of sign it is. All speed limit signs are the same shape and color. Lidar can detect the shape, but a camera is needed to sense the color (and read the speed limit itself).

Making Improvements

One way to improve self-driving cars is to improve the roads they drive on. Imagine if roads could communicate with your car. A company called 3M is doing just that. 3M is the country's biggest manufacturer of road signs and even the paint used for lines on roads. They have begun

Bad weather conditions are very difficult for self-driving cars to drive in.

experimenting with adding different types of

metal to this paint that car sensors can detect.

Self-driving cars are being tested every day.

The technology continues to get better. Even

though self-driving cars are far less likely to make

mistakes than human drivers, it may take people a while to become comfortable with them. Brave people will need to lead

When you are an adult, you will most likely use a self-driving car.

the way for others by riding in self-driving cars. Will you be one of those people?

FAST FACT

One thing that humans can do better than self-driving cars is drive in bad weather! It's really tough for a self-driving car to know how to handle rain, ice, and snow. This is one area in which humans still have an advantage—for now.

TECHNOLOGY TIMELINE

1500s Leonardo da Vinci draws plans for a
self-propelled cart.

1939 Norman Bel Geddes shows his exhibition
"Futurama" at the 1939 World's Fair.

1958 RCA and General Motors develop a car that can
sense electrical signals from a special wire in
the road.

1979 After two decades of work, Stanford University
tests a cart with a camera and
self-driving capabilities.

2016 Google turns its self-driving car unit into a
separate company, Waymo.

GLOSSARY

assistive Something designed to help a person do a task.

autonomy The ability to control one's own actions.

echolocation The method of navigation used by some animals, like dolphins. The animal sends out a sound. If the sound bounces off a nearby object, the animal can determine the object's location.

GPS "Global Positioning System." A series of satellites orbiting Earth, which help objects determine their location on Earth.

lidar "Light Detection and Ranging." A system that uses laser pulses to detect the location of objects.

orbit To float around an object, maintaining the same distance from the object at all times.

sonar "Sound Navigation and Ranging." A system for locating objects using sound waves.

FIND OUT MORE

BOOKS

Currie, Stephen. *Self-Driving Car*. Tech Bytes. Chicago:
Norwood House Press, 2016.

Marsico, Katie. *Self-Driving Cars*. A True Book. New York:
Scholastic, 2016.

WEBSITES

How Stuff Works

https://auto.howstuffworks.com/under-the-hood/
trends-innovations/driverless-car.htm

Mocomi

http://mocomi.com/driverless-cars

INDEX

ABOUT THE AUTHOR

Ian Chow-Miller is a robotics and engineering middle-school teacher. He is a member of the LEGO Education Advisory Panel and is a constant contributor to Tufts University's LEGO Engineering website. Ian coaches robotics and soccer teams after school. He is married to an awesome wife and has two great sons who are budding artists and engineers.